A Woman's Mission

by

John Angell James

Author of
A Help to Domestic Happiness, Addresses to Young Men,
The Christian Father's Present to His Children,
The Widow Directed to the Widow's God,
and *Female Piety*

Edited by Dr. Don Kistler

Soli Deo Gloria Publications
. . . for instruction in righteousness . . .

Soli Deo Gloria Publications
P. O. Box 451, Morgan, PA 15064
(412) 221-1901/FAX 22-1902
www.SDGbooks.com

*

A Woman's Mission is excerpted from the book
Female Piety, published by Soli Deo Gloria.
© 1999

*

ISBN 1-57358-117-8

A Woman's Mission

"And the Lord God said, 'It is not good that the man should be alone. I will make him an help meet for him.' "
Genesis 2:18

"What in the great, diversified, and busy world is my place and my business?" is a question which everyone should ask. For everyone has a place to fill and a part to act. And to act his part well, according to the will of God, in the lofty drama of human life, should be the ambition, solicitude, and prayer of each of us. It is the first lesson of wisdom to know our place, the second to keep it—and, of course, corresponding to this, to ascertain the duties of our place and to discharge them. There are class duties as well as individual ones, and the latter are generally to be more accurately learned by an intelligent apprehension of the former. Woman, as such, has her mission. What is it? What is precisely the rank she is to occupy? What is the purpose she is to fulfill, above which she would be unduly exalted, and below which she would be unjustly degraded? This is a subject which should be thoroughly understood in order that she may know what to claim, and man what to concede; that she may know what she has to do, and that he may know what he has a right to expect.

I shall endeavor to answer this question, and point out the nature of woman's mission. In doing this, I shall consult the infallible oracle of Scripture, and not the speculations of moralists, economists, and philosophers. I hold this to be our rule in the matter before us. God is the Creator of both sexes, the constructor of society, the author of social relations, and the arbiter of social duties, claims, and immunities. And this is admitted by all who believe in the authority of the Bible. You are content, my female friends, to abide by the decisions of this oracle. You have every reason to be so. He who created you is best qualified to declare the intention of His own acts, and you may safely, as you should humbly, allow Him to fix your position and make known your duties. In common with man, woman has a heavenly calling to glorify God as the end of her existence, and to perform all the duties and enjoy all the blessings of a religious life. Like man, she is a sinful, rational, and immortal creature, placed under an economy of mercy, and called, by repentance towards God and faith in our Lord Jesus Christ, to eternal life. Religion is as much her vocation as that of the other sex. In Christ Jesus there is neither male nor female, but all are on the same level as to obligations, duties, and privileges.

In common with man, she is called, where she is unmarried and dependent, to labor for her own support—a condition to which large portions of the community are necessarily subject by the circumstances of their birth. Industry is as incumbent upon her as upon the other sex, and indolence is as inexcusable in her as in man. But in the married state, her sphere of labor, as we shall presently show, is her family; and it belongs to the husband to earn by the sweat of his brow not only his own bread, but that of the household. In many of the uncivilized tribes, where the ameliorating condition of Christianity is not felt, the wife is the drudge of the family while the husband lives in lordly sloth; and even in this country, at least in its manufacturing portions, manual labor falls too often and too heavily upon married women, greatly to the detriment of their families. An unmarried woman, however, without fortune, must provide for herself in some way or other, according to the circumstances of her birth and situation; and let her not consider herself degraded by it. Honest industry is far more honorable than pride and sloth.

But neither of these is the peculiar mission of woman, as pertaining to her sex. To know what this is, we must, as I have said, consult the pages of revelation, and ascertain the declared motive of God for her creation. "And the Lord God said, 'It is not good that the man should be alone; I will make him an help meet for him.' " This is further expressed, or rather repeated, where it is said, "And Adam," or "Although Adam had given names to all cattle, and to the fowl of the air, and to every beast of the field, yet for Adam there was not found an help meet for him." Nothing can be more clear from this than that woman was made for man. Adam was created as a being with undeveloped social propensities, which indeed seem essential to all creatures. It is the sublime peculiarity of deity to be entirely independent, for happiness, of all other beings. He, and He only, is the theater of His own glory, the fountain of His own felicity, and a sufficient object of His own contemplation, needing nothing for His bliss but self-communion. An archangel alone in heaven would pine, even there, for some companionship, either divine or angelic.

Adam, surrounded by all the glories of Paradise, and by all the various tribes it contained, found himself alone and needing companionship. Without it his life was but a solitude, Eden itself a desert. Endowed with a nature too communicative to be satisfied from himself alone, he sighed for society, for support, for some complement to his existence, and only half-lived so long as he lived alone. Formed to think, to speak, to love, his thoughts yearned for other thoughts with which to compare and exercise his soaring aspirations. His words were wearisomely wasted upon the wanton air, or at best awoke but an echo which mocked instead of answering him. His love, as regards an earthly object, knew not where to bestow itself, and, returning to his own bosom, threatened to degenerate into a desolating egotism. His entire being longed, in short, for another self, but that other self did not exist; there was no help meet for him. The visible creatures which surrounded him were too much beneath him, and the invisible Being who gave him life was too much above him, to unite their condition with his own. Whereupon God made woman, and the great problem was immediately solved.

It was, then, the characteristic of unfallen man to want someone to sympathize with him in his joys, as it is of fallen man to want someone to sympathize with him in his sorrows. Whether Adam was so far conscious of his wants as to ask for a companion we are not informed. It would appear from the inspired record as if the design of this precious boon originated with God, and as if Eve, like so many of His other mercies, was the spontaneous bestowment of His own free will. Thus Adam would have to say, as did one of his most illustrious descendants many ages afterwards, "Thou preventest me with Thy goodness."

Here, then, is the design of God in creating woman: to be a suitable helpmate to man. Man needed a companion, and God gave him woman. And as there was no other man than Adam at that time in existence, Eve was designed exclusively for Adam's comfort. This teaches us from the beginning that whatever mission woman may have to accomplish in reference to man, in a generic sense, her mission, at least in wedded life, is to be a suitable helpmate for that one man to whom she is united. It was declared from the beginning that every other tie, though not severed by marriage, shall be rendered subordinate, and a man shall "leave his father and mother and cleave unto his wife, and they two shall be one flesh."

If woman's mission in Paradise was to be man's companion and joy, such must be the case still. Her vocation has not been changed by the Fall. By that catastrophe, man needs still more urgently a companion, and God has rendered this mission of hers still more explicit by the declaration, "Thy desire shall be to thy husband and he shall rule over thee." It has been often shown that by being taken from himself, she was equal to man in nature; while the very part of the body from which she was abstracted indicated the position she was intended to occupy. She was not taken from the head, to show she was not to rule over him; nor from his foot, to teach that she was not to be his slave; nor from his hand, to show that she was not to be his tool; but from his side, to show that she was to be his companion. There may perhaps be more of ingenuity and fancy in this than of God's original design; but if a mere conceit, it is at once both pardonable and instructive.

That woman was intended to occupy a position of subordination and dependence is clear from every part of the Word of God. This is declared in language already quoted: "Thy desire shall be to thy husband, and he shall rule over thee." This referred not only to Eve personally, but to Eve representatively. It was the divine law of the relation of the sexes, then promulgated for all time. The preceding language placed woman, as a punishment for her sin, in a state of sorrow; this places her in a state of subjection. Her husband was to be the center of her earthly desires, and, to a certain extent, the regulator of them also; and she was to be in subjection to him. What was enacted in Paradise has been confirmed by every subsequent dispensation of grace. Judaism is full of it in all its provisions; and Christianity equally establishes it.

I shall here introduce and explain the words of the apostle: "I would have you to know that the head of every man is Christ, and the head of the woman is the man." He then goes on to direct that women should not, unveiled and with their hair cut off, exercise the miraculous gifts which were sometimes bestowed upon them, and adds, "A man indeed ought not to cover his head, forasmuch as he is the image and glory of God; but the woman is the glory of the man. Neither was the man created for the woman, but the woman for the man." For the explanation of this passage, I remark that in the times of the apostles there were two recognized characteristic emblems of the female sex when they appeared in public: veils and the preservation of their tresses. It would seem from the apostle's remarks as if some of the female members of the Corinthian church, during the time when the inspiration of the Holy Spirit was upon them, cast off their veils after the manner of the heathen priestesses when they delivered the responses of the oracles. This conduct the apostle reproves, and informs them that if the veil were thrown aside they might as well also cut off their flowing hair, which is one of woman's distinctions from man, and is by all nations considered the ornament as well as the peculiarity of the sex.

We may pause for a moment to observe how constantly and completely Christianity is the parent of order, and the enemy of indecorum of every kind. Why were not the women to lay aside their veils? Because it would be forgetting their subordination and dependence, and assuming an equal rank with man. This is the gist of the apostle's reason. It was not merely indecorous and contrary to modesty, but it was ambitious and violated the order of heaven. The other expressions of the apostle in this passage are very strong. As Christ is the head or ruler of man, so man is the head and ruler of woman in the domestic economy. Man was made to show forth God's glory and praise, to be in subordination to Him and only to Him; woman was created to be, in addition to this, the glory of man by being in subordination to him, as his help and his ornament. She was not only made *out of* him, but *for* him. All her loveliness, comeliness, and purity are not only the expressions of her excellence, but of his honor and dignity, since all were not only derived from him, but made for him.

This, then, is woman's true position, and if anything more need be said to prove it from the records of Christianity we may refer to apostolic language in other places, where wives are enjoined to "be subject to their husbands in all things, even as the church is subject to Christ." Nor is the Apostle Paul alone in this, for Peter writes in the same strain. Let woman then bow to this authority, and not feel herself degraded by such submission. It has been said that in domestic life man shines as the sun, but woman as the moon, with a splendor borrowed from the man. It may be said with greater truth and propriety, and less invidiously, that man shines as the primary planet, reflecting the glory of God, who is the center of the moral universe, and woman, while she equally derives her splendor from the central Luminary and is governed by His attraction, is yet the satellite of man, revolves around him, follows him in his course, and ministers to him.

Behold, then, I say again, woman's position and mission is summed up in love and subjection to her husband. Everything connected with the relationship of man and woman has, however, since the Fall, a more serious character; her love has become more anxious; her humility more profound. Bashful of her own defects, and anxious to reinstate herself in her husband's heart, woman lives to repair the wrong she has inflicted on man, and lavishes upon him consolations which may sweeten the present bitterness of sin, and warnings which may preserve from the future bitterness of hell.

Woman, then, whatever relation she may bear to society at large, whatever duties in consequence of this relation she may have to discharge, and whatever benefits by the right discharge of these duties she may have it in her power to confer upon the community, must consider herself chiefly called to advance the comfort of man in his private relations; to promote her own

peace by promoting his; and to receive from him all that respect, protection, and ever assiduous affection to which her
equal nature, her companionship, and her devotedness give her
so just a claim. She is, in wedded life, to be his constant companion, in whose society he is to find one who meets him
hand to hand, eye to eye, lip to lip, and heart to heart; to
whom he can unburden the secrets of a heart pressed down
with care or wrung with anguish; whose presence shall be to
him better than all society; whose voice shall be his sweetest
music, whose smiles his brightest sunshine; from whom he
shall go forth with regret, and to whose converse he shall re-
turn with willing feet when the toils of the day are over; who
shall walk near his loving heart, and feel the throbbing of affection as her arm leans on his and presses on his side. In his
hours of retired conversation, he shall tell her all the secrets of
his heart, find in her all the capabilities and all the promptings
of the most tender and endeared fellowship, and in her gentle
smiles and unrestrained speech enjoy all to be expected in one
who was given by God to be his associate and friend.

In that companionship which woman was designed to af-
ford to man must of course be included the sympathetic offices
of the comforter. It is her role, in their hours of retirement, to
console and cheer him; when he is injured or insulted, to heal
the wounds of his troubled spirit; when he burdened by care, to
lighten his load by sharing it; when he groaning with anguish,
to calm by her peace-speaking words the tumult of his heart,
and to act, in all his sorrows, the part of a ministering angel.

Nor should she be backward to offer, nor he backward to
receive, the counsels of wisdom which her prudence will suggest, even though she may not be intimately acquainted with
all the entanglements of this world's business. Woman's advice,
had it been asked for and acted upon, would have saved thou-
sands of men from bankruptcy and ruin. Few men have ever

had to regret their taking counsel from a prudent wife, while multitudes have had to reproach themselves for their folly in not asking, and multitudes more for not following, the counsels of such a companion.

If, then, this is woman's mission according to the representation of her Almighty Creator, to be the suitable helpmate of that man to whom she has given herself as the companion of his pilgrimage upon earth, it of course supposes that marriage, contracted with a due regard to prudence and under all proper regulations, is the natural state of both man and woman. And so, I affirm, in truth it is. Providence has willed it and nature prompts it. But as the exceptions are so numerous, is there no mission for those to whom the exception appertains? Is it married women only who have a mission, and an important one? Certainly not. In these cases, I fall back upon woman's mission to society at large. And is not this momentous? Has it not been admitted in all ages, and by all countries, that the influence of female character upon social virtue and happiness, and upon national strength and prosperity, is prodigious, whether for good or for evil? Is not the declaration with which Adolphe Monod opens his beautiful treatise perfectly true? "The greatest influence on earth, whether for good or for evil, is possessed by woman. Let us study the history of bygone ages, the state of barbarism and civilization; of the east and the west; of Paganism and Christianity; of antiquity and the middle ages; of the medieval and modern times; and we shall find that there is nothing which more decidedly separates them than the condition of woman." Every woman, whether rich or poor, married or single, has a circle of influence within which, according to her character, she is exerting a certain amount of power for good or harm. Every woman, by her virtue or her vice, by her folly or her wisdom, by her levity or her dignity, is adding something to our national elevation or degradation. As long as female virtue is prevalent, upheld by one sex and respected by the other, a nation cannot sink very low in the scale of ignominy by plunging into the depths of vice.

To a certain extent, woman is the conservator of her nation's welfare. Her virtue, if firm and uncorrupted, will stand sentinel over that of the empire. Law, justice, liberty, and the arts all contribute, of course, to the well-being of a nation; beneficial influence flows in from various springs, and innumerable contributors may be at work, each laboring in his vocation for his country's weal. But let the general tone of female morals be low, and all will be rendered nugatory, while, on the other hand, the universal prevalence of womanly intelligence and virtue will swell the stream of civilization to its highest level, impregnate it with its richest qualities, and spread its fertility over the widest surface. A community is not likely to be overthrown where woman fulfills her mission, for by the power of her noble heart over the hearts of others she will raise it from its ruins and restore it again to prosperity and joy. Here, then, beyond the circle of wedded life as well as within it, is no doubt part of woman's mission, and an important one it is. Her field is social life, her object is social happiness, her reward is social gratitude and respect.

"If any female," says Mr. Upham in his life of Madame Guyon, "should think these pages worthy of her perusal, let her gather the lesson from these statements, that woman's influence does not terminate, as is sometimes supposed, with the molding and the guidance of the minds of children; her task is not finished when she sends abroad those whom she has borne and nurtured in her bosom, on their pilgrimage of action and duty in this wide world. Far from it. Man is neither safe in himself, nor profitable to others, when he lives dissociated from that benign influence which is to be found in woman's presence and character—an influence which is needed in the projects and toils of mature life, in the temptations and trials to which that period is especially exposed, and in the weakness and sufferings of age, hardly less than in childhood and youth.

"But it is not the woman who is gay, frivolous, and unbelieving, or woman separated from those divine teachings which make all hearts wise, that can lay claim to the exercise of such an influence. But when she adds to the traits of sympathy, forbearance, and warm affection which characterize her the strength and wisdom of a well-cultivated intellect, and the still higher attributes of religious faith and holy love, it is not easy to limit the good she may do in all situations, and in all periods of life."

If I am right as to the nature of woman's mission, I cannot err as to the proper sphere of it. If she was created for man, and not only for the race of man, but for one man, then the easy and necessary inference is that home is the proper scene of woman's action and influence. There are few terms in the language around which cluster so many blissful associations as that delight of every English heart, the word "home." The elysium of love, the nursery of virtue, the garden of enjoyment, the temple of concord, the circle of all tender relationships, the playground of childhood, the dwelling of manhood, the retreat of age; where health loves to enjoy its pleasures, wealth revels in its luxuries, and poverty bears its rigors; where sickness can best endure its pains, and dissolving nature expire; which throws its spell over those who are within its charmed circle, and even sends its attractions across oceans and continents, drawing to itself the thoughts and wishes of the man who wanders from it to the antipodes—this home, sweet home is the sphere of wedded woman's mission.

Is it any hardship upon woman, any depreciation of her importance, to place her sphere of action and influence there? Is it to assign her a circle of influence unworthy of herself if we call her to preside over that little community of which home is the seat? Can we estimate the importance of such a scene of action? Shall we tell of the varied and momentous interests which are included in that circle? Shall we speak of the happiness of a husband whose bliss, to so considerable an extent, is created by her, and involves her own, or the character and future well-being (for both worlds) of children, if she has them? Or the comfort of servants, and the order and pleasant working of the whole domestic constitution, all which depend so much upon her? Why, to make one such home a seat of holiness and happiness, to fill one such sphere with an influence so sweet and sacred, to throw the fascination of connubial feeling and of maternal influence over one such community, to irradiate so many countenances with delight, to fill so many hearts with contentment, and to prepare so many characters for their future part in life—such an object would be deemed by an angel worth an incarnation upon earth.

Or from this sense of her duties shall we look abroad upon the public good, the strength and stability of the nation? Who knows not that the springs of an empire's prosperity lie in its domestic constitution, and in well-trained families? Even one such family is a contribution to the majestic flow of a nation's greatness. Can such families exist without a woman's care, oversight, and wisdom? Has it not grown into a proverb that home has ever been the nursery of great men, and their mothers their instructresses? It may be said as a general principle that woman is not only the mother of the body, but of the character of her children. To her is first entrusted the instruction of the mind, the cultivation of the heart, and the formation of the life. Thought, feeling, will, imagination, virtue, religion, or the contrary moral tendencies all germinate under her fostering influence. The greatest power in the moral world is that which a mother exercises over her young child. The decisive moment in education is the starting point. The dominant direction which is to determine the whole course of life lies concealed in the first years of infancy; and these belong to the mother.

One of the most hallowed, lovely, and beautiful sights in our world is a woman at home discharging, in all the meekness of wisdom, the various duties of wife, mother, and mistress, with an order that nothing is allowed to disturb, a patience which nothing can exhaust, an affection which is never ruffled, and a perseverance that no difficulties can interrupt, nor any disappointments arrest—in short, such a scene as that described by the writer of the most exquisite chapter of the Proverbs. Eve in Paradise, in all her untainted loveliness, by the side of Adam, propping the lily, training the vine, or directing the growth of the rose—shedding upon him, and receiving, reflected back from his noble countenance upon her happy spirit, such smiles as told in silent language their perfect and conjoint bliss—was, no doubt, a brighter image of perfect virtue and undisturbed felicity. But to me, a woman in our fallen world, guiding in piety, intelligence, and all matronly and motherly excellences the circle of a home made happy chiefly by her influence, presents a scene little inferior in beauty, and far superior as a display of virtue and intelligence, to that of which our first mother was the center even in her original perfections. And it is fancy, and not reason and moral taste, that can revel in the mind's pictures of Eve in Paradise, and not feel warmer admiration in the actual presence of such a woman as I have described.

But it will, perhaps, be asked whether I would shut up every married woman within the domestic circle, and, with the jealousy and authority of an oriental despot, confine her to her own home, or whether I would condemn and degrade her to mere household drudgery. I have, I think, protected myself already from this imputation by representing her as the companion, counselor, and comforter of man. She shall never, with my consent, sink from the side of man to be trampled under his feet. She shall not have one ray of her glory extinguished, nor be deprived of a single honor that belongs to her sex. To be the instructress of her children, the companion of her husband, and the queen consort of the domestic state is no degradation; and she only is degraded who thinks so.

Still in connection with—though not in neglect of—this, let her give her influence upon society to the circle of her friends on all suitable occasions and in all suitable places. Though the drawing room is not the chief sphere of her influence, it is one of the circles in which she may move; and although incessant parties of pleasure, and a constant round of entertainments, are not her mission, but oppose and hinder it, yet she is occasionally to bestow that influence which every wise and good woman exerts over the tone of morals and manners among the friends who may court her society. Woman is the grace, ornament, and charm of the social circle; and when she carries into it habits that frown upon vice, that check folly and discountenance levity, she is a benefactress to the country. And as to the various institutions of our age for the relief of suffering humanity, the instruction of ignorance, and the spread of religion, we give her all the room and liberty for these things which are compatible with her duties to her own household. What prudent female would ask more, or what advocate of her rights would claim more? Woman is always in her place where charity presides, except when her time and attention are demanded at home for those who are more immediately her charge. But I shall have much more to urge on this subject in a future chapter.

But what shall I say of those women who claim on their own behalf, or of their advocates who claim for them, a participation in the labors, occupations, rights, and duties which have usually been considered as exclusively appertaining to men? There are those who would expunge the line of demarcation which nearly all nations have drawn between the duties and occupations of men and those of women. Christianity has provided a place for woman for which she is fitted and in which she shines; but take her out of that place, and her luster pales and sheds a feeble and sickly ray. Or, to change the metaphor, woman is a plant, which in the seclusion of its own greenhouse will put forth all its brilliant colors and all its sweet perfume; but if you remove it from the protection of its own floral home into the common garden and open field, where hardier flowers will grow and thrive, its beauty fades and its odor is diminished. Neither reason nor Christianity invites woman to the professor's chair, conducts her to the bar, makes her welcome to the pulpit, or admits her to the place of ordinary magistracy. Both exclude her, not indeed by positive and specific commands, but by general principles and spirit, alike from the violence and license of the camp, the debates of the senate, and the pleadings of the forum. And they bid her beware how she lays aside the delicacy of her sex and listens to any doctrines which claim new rights for her, and becomes the dupe of those who have put themselves forward as her advocates only to gain notoriety or perhaps bread. They forbid us to hear her gentle voice in the popular assembly, and do not even suffer her to speak in the Church of God. They claim not for her the right of suffrage, nor any immunity by which she may "usurp authority over the man." The Bible gives her her place of majesty and dignity in the domestic circle—the heart of her husband and the heart of her family. It is the female supremacy of that domain where love, tenderness, refinement, thought, and feeling preside. It is the privilege of making her husband happy and honored, and her sons and daughters the ornaments

of human society. It is the sphere of piety, prudence, diligence
in the domestic station, and a holy and devout life. It is the
sphere that was occupied by Hannah, the mother of Samuel;
by Elizabeth, the mother of John; by Eunice, the mother of
Timothy; and by Mary, the mother of Jesus. It is the respect
and esteem of mankind. It is that silent, unobserved, unobtru-
sive influence by which she accomplishes more for her race
than many whose names occupy a broad space on the page of
history.

A woman who fills well the sphere assigned to her as a
good wife, a mother, and a mistress—who trains up good citi-
zens for the state, and good fathers and mothers of other families which are to spring from her own, and so from generation
to generation in all but endless succession—need not complain
that her sphere of action and her power of influence are too
limited for female ambition to aspire to. The mothers of the
wise and the good are the benefactresses of their species. What
would be gained as for woman's comfort, respectability, or
usefulness, or for the welfare of society, and how much would
be lost to each by withdrawing her from her own appropriate
sphere and introducing her to that for which she has no adaptation? Who but a few wild visionaries, rash speculators, and
mistaken advocates of woman's rights would take her from the
home of her husband, of her children, and of her own heart,
to wear out her strength, consume her time, and destroy her
feminine excellence in committee rooms, on platforms, and in
mechanics' or philosophical institutions?

But may not woman, in every way in her power, benefit
society by her talents and her influence? Certainly, in every
legitimate way. Her sphere is clearly assigned to her by
Providence, and only by very special and obvious calls should
she be induced to leave it. Whatever breaks down the modest
reserve, the domestic virtues, or the persuasive gentleness of

woman is an injury done to the community. Woman can be spared from the lecturer's chair, the platform of general convocation, and the scene of public business; but she cannot be spared from the hearth of her husband and the circle of her children. Substitutes can be found for her in the one, but not in the other. In the bosom of domestic privacy she fulfills with truest dignity and faithfulness the first and highest obligations of her sex.

Monod's remarks on this subject are so beautiful, appropriate, and just that I shall be more than forgiven for the following quotation:

> Is not the humble sphere which we assign to woman precisely that for which her whole being is predisposed and pre-constituted? Her finer but more fragile conformation, the quicker pulsation of her heart, the more exquisite sensibility of her nerves, the delicacy of her organs, and even the softness of her features, all combine to make her what St. Peter so aptly designates "the weaker vessel," and render her constitutionally unfit for incessant and weighty cares, for the duties of the state, for the vigils of the cabinet, for all that which yields renown in the world.
>
> Again, are not the powers of her mind equally distinct? The question is sometimes raised whether they are equal to those of man. They are neither equal nor unequal; they are different, being wisely adapted to another end. For the accomplishment of the work assigned to man, woman's faculties are inferior to his; or rather she is not adapted to it. We speak of the general rule, and not of exceptions. It must be conceded that, by way of exception, there are among women some few whose intellects are adapted to the cares reserved, on principle, to the other sex, and that peculiar situations may arise in which women of ordinary capacities may be called upon to discharge the duties assigned to man, man in that case being a defaulter; it must be seen,

however, that these exceptions are clearly indicated by God, or called for by the interests of humanity. For, after all, in the mission of woman, humility is but the means, charity the end, to which all must be subservient. And why should not God, who has made exceptions of this nature in sacred history, do the same in ordinary life?

Be this as it may, we leave exceptions to God, and to the conscience of the individual, and, abstaining from all irritating, personal, or contestable questions, will confine ourselves simply to the general rule.

Generally speaking, enlarged views of politics and science, the bold flight of metaphysics, the sublimer conceptions of poetry, which, bursting every shackle, soar in the boundless regions of thought and imagination, are not in the province of woman.

In that limited sphere, however, of which we are speaking, limited in extent, but boundless in influence, within which, supported by Scripture, we exhort woman to confine her actions, she is endowed with faculties superior to those of man, or rather, she alone is adapted to it. Here she has her requital; here she proves herself mistress of the field, and employs those secret resources (which might be termed admirable, if they did not inspire a more tender sentiment both towards her and towards God, who has so richly endowed her): her practical survey, equally sure and rapid; her quick and accurate perception; her wonderful power of penetrating the heart, in a way unknown and impracticable to man; her never-failing presence of mind and personal attention on all occasions; her constant though imperceptible vigilance; her numerous and fertile resources in the management of her domestic affairs; her ever-ready access and willing audience to all who need her; her freedom of thought and action in the midst of the most agonizing sufferings and accumulated embarrassments; her elasticity (may I say her perseverance?) despite her feebleness; her exquisitely tender feelings; her tact that would seem so practiced, were it not instinctive; her extreme perfection in little things; her dexterous industry in the work of her hands; her incomparable skill in nursing the sick, in cheering a broken spirit, in reawakening a sleeping conscience, in reopening a heart that has long been closed—in sum, innumerable are the things which she accomplishes, and which man can neither discern nor effect, without the aid of her eye and hand.

Milton has finely expressed the difference between the original pair:

> *For contemplation he, and valour formed;*
> *For softness she, and sweet attractive grace.*

And this difference, by limiting their respective capacities, prescribes their separate duties and spheres of action.

Now look at woman's natural adaptation for her sphere. If the view here given of woman's mission is correct, we can in a moment perceive what is required to enable her to fulfill it. There must be, as indeed there generally is pervading the sex, a consciousness of subordination, without any sense of degradation or any wish that it was otherwise. Woman scarcely needs to be taught that in the domestic economy she is second and not first, that "the man is the head of the woman." This is a law of nature written on the heart, and coincides exactly with the law of God written on the pages of revelation. It is, first of all, an instinct, and then confirmed by reason. Without this law deeply engraved and constantly felt as well as known, her situation would be endured as a slavery, and she would be constantly endeavoring to throw off the yoke. Her condition would be wretched, and she would make all wretched around her. With such a sense of oppression, or even of hardship, pressing upon the mind, no duty could be well performed, and the family would be a scene of domestic warfare. But she generally knows her place, and feels it is her happiness as well as her duty to keep it. It is not necessity, but even choice that produces a willing subjection. She is contented that it should be so, for God has implanted the disposition in her nature.

Then her gentleness is another part of her qualification for her duty. She should have, must have, really has, influence and power of impulsion, if not compulsion. Were she utterly powerless, she could do nothing. Her influence, however, is a kind of passive power; it is the power that draws rather than drives, and commands by obeying. Her gentleness makes her strong. How winning are her smiles, how melting her tears, how insinuating her words! Woman loses her power when she parts from her gentleness. It is this very yielding, like the bulrush lifting its head after the rush of water to which it has bowed, that gives her a power to rise superior to the force of circumstances which, if resistance were offered, would break all before them. She vanquishes by submission. How necessary gentleness is to the fulfillment of her mission in handling the young and tender spirits of her children, in training the first delicate shoots of their infant dispositions, and for directing the feelings of that one heart on which she depends for her happiness. There are many varieties of disposition in women, which may make them sensitive, petulant, irritable, jealous, quick to feel and to resent; but notwithstanding all this, and under all this, there is a gentleness of disposition which indicates this vocation as destined to influence and constrain by love.

Tenderness is another of her characteristics. Gentleness relates more to manner, tenderness more to disposition; the former to habitual conduct towards all persons and all cases, this one to the occasional exercise of sympathy with distress. Tenderness is so characteristic of the female heart that an unfeeling woman is considered a libel upon her sex. If compassion were driven out from every other habitation, it would find there its last retreat. Her heart is so made of tenderness that she is ever in danger of being imposed upon by craft and false-hood. How suitable such a disposition for one who is to be the chief comforter of the domestic commonwealth; who is to mollify the wounds of her husband's heart, and to heal the sorrows of her children; whose ear is to listen to every tale of domestic woe, and whose bosom is to be the lodging place of all the family's grief!

Self-denial is no less necessary for this domestic mission than anything I have yet mentioned. How much ease, com-fort, and enjoyment must she surrender who has to consult her husband's comfort and will before her own; whose happiness is to consist, in a great measure, in making others happy; who has first to endure all that is connected with giving birth to her children, and then all that is involved in nursing, watching, comforting, and training them! One of the most striking in-stances in our world of endurance and self-denial, both as to the extent and the cheerfulness with which it is borne, is the busy, tender, and contented mother of a growing family. God has given the power, yet I sometimes wonder how she can ex-ercise it.

And then see her fortitude in this situation. In that courage which leads man to the cannon's mouth, to mount the breach, or to encounter some terrific danger of any other kind, she is inferior to man; but in the fortitude manifested by enduring bodily suffering, the ills of poverty, the wasting influ-ence of long-continued privations, the gloom of solitude, the bitterness of injustice, the cruelty of neglect, and the misery of oppression, is she not in all these as superior to man as man is to her in all that pertains to brute force?

On the subject of woman's fortitude and power of endurance, I will introduce, though it may be at some length, the most surprising instance of it perhaps on record, whether in inspired or uninspired history, and it will serve as an appropriate illustration of this part of the subject of the chapter. The Apostle John, in his narrative of the events of the crucifixion of our Lord, says with beautiful simplicity, and without a single comment, as if he could not hope and would not attempt to add to the grandeur of the incident: "Now there stood by the cross of Jesus His mother, and His mother's sister, Mary the wife of Cleophas, and Mary Magdalene." That the other women should have been there is less wonderful, though even their presence at such a scene (from which it would seem as if all the apostles had retired except John) was indeed an instance of the fortitude of heroic love. But that His mother should have been there, not far off but beside the cross, not prostrate in a swoon or beating her breast, wringing her hands, tearing her hair, and shrieking in frantic grief, but standing in silent, though pensive, anguish to witness the horrors of crucifixion, so far surpassing those of any modern method of execution; the crucifixion of her Son, and such a Son—oh, wondrous woman! an act surpassing wonder! To whatever length endurance may be carried by attendance at the sickbed of a dying friend, how few of even female heroes could witness the execution of a husband, son, or brother.

I have read of one who, when her lover was executed for high treason, went in a mourning coach to witness the dreadful process, and when the whole was closed by the severing of that head which had leaned on her bosom, simply said, "I follow thee," and, sighing forth his name, fell back in the coach and instantly expired. Here was a power of endurance carried to a point which nature could sustain no longer, and it sunk at length, crushed beneath the intolerable burden of its grief. But behold the scene before us: that mother, in the dignity and majesty of profound, yet composed grief, enduring to the end. Peter had denied his Master; the other disciples, at the sight of the officers of justice and the soldiers, amidst the deep shadows of Gethsemane, had deserted Him, and still kept at a distance from the scene of suffering and danger. But there, standing by the cross, were those dauntless, holy women, sustaining with wondrous fortitude the sight of His dying agonies, and confessing their Lord in the hour of His deepest humiliation, in the absence of His friends and in the presence of His foes—and there among them was His mother. I shall never wonder at anything that female fortitude, when upheld by divine grace, can do after it could stand in the person of Mary at the foot of the cross, when Christ, her Son and her Lord, was suspended upon it. Nor shall I ever despair of the support of any woman, in the hour and scene of her deepest woe, who is willing to be sustained after I have beheld the mother of our Lord upheld in that unutterably awful situation.

Painters and poets have not done justice to the dignity of this most honored of all women. There is a picture of Annibale Carracci's entitled "The Three Marys," the subject of which is those holy women surveying the body of Christ after it was taken down from the cross. As a work of art it is inimitable, and does full justice to the painter's skill. But it does far less justice to the character of the mother of our Lord than the apostle's description of her. In the painting she is represented swooning over the dead body of Jesus, whose head reclines on her lap, while the other figures are represented in the attitude of passionate grief. How different this is from the dignified, majestic, and composed grief which stood beneath the cross. So far must art ever fall beneath nature, still lower below the wonders of grace, and most of all below such grace as was vouchsafed to the mother of our Lord.

Let females study this pathetic and amazing scene, and

learn that the deepest love and the noblest grief are not that sickly sensibility, that emotional excitability, which are too tender to bear the sight of suffering, but that which, instead of sinking with hysterical outcries, retiring with averted eyes from agonies, or swooning at the sight of tears and blood, can control the feelings and brace the nerves to perform in the hour and scene of woe a part which none can perform except herself, or at any rate none can perform so well. Let young women set out in life practicing that discipline of their emotions which, without diminishing all of that softness and tenderness of manner which are the most lovely characteristics of their sex, or robbing their hearts of those delicate sympathies and sensibilities which constitute the glory of woman's nature, will preserve their judgment from being enveloped in such a mist of feeling, and their will from being so enervated, as to make them incapable of resolution and render them incompetent in times of their own sorrow and trial for anything besides weeping over the calamities which they might otherwise remove, and to make them altogether unfit for those hardy services of mercy which the miseries of others will sometimes require at their hands.

Arising out of this self-discipline, and as one beautiful display of it, see woman when called to put forth her gentleness, her sympathy, and her self-denial in the hour of affliction and the chamber of sickness. It has been somewhere beautifully said that "In sickness there is no hand like woman's hand, no heart like woman's heart." A man's breast may swell with unquestionable sorrow, and apprehension may rend his mind; yet place him by the sick couch, and in the light (or I should rather say in the shadow) of the sad lamp by which it is watched; let him have to count over the long dull hours of night, and await, alone and sleepless, the grey dawn struggling into the chamber of suffering; let him be appointed to this ministry, even for the sake of the brother of his heart or the father of his being—and his grosser nature, even when most perfect, will tire, his eye will close, and his spirit will grow impatient of the dreary task. And though his love and anxiety remain undiminished, his mind will experience a creeping in of irresistible selfishness, which indeed he may be ashamed of and struggle to reject, but which, despite all his efforts, will remain to characterize his nature, and prove in one respect, at least, the weakness of man. But see a mother, a sister, or a wife in his place! The woman feels no weariness, and has no thought of herself. In silence and in the depth of night, she bears up not only passively, but (so far as the term, with the necessary qualification, may express our meaning) with delight. Her ear acquires a blind man's instinct, as from time to time it catches the slightest stir, whisper, or breath of the now more-than-ever loved one who lies under the hand of human affliction. Her step, as she moves in obedience to an impulse or signal, would not awaken a mouse; if she speaks, her accents are a soft echo of natural harmony, most delicious to the sick man's ear, conveying all that sound can convey of pity, comfort, and devotion. And thus, night after night, she tends him like a creature sent from a higher world, when all earthly watchfulness has failed; her eye never winking, her mind never palled, her nature, which at all other times is weakness, now gaining a superhuman strength and magnanimity, herself forgotten, and her sex alone predominant.

But as woman's mission is, in a special sense, one of charity, love is, above all things, essential to its right performance. Here again, I will give a long quotation from Monod's beautiful work:

> But in speaking of love, it is less the degree than the character which is of importance. Love, as we have

before said, is the very essence of woman's existence. But what love? Let her reflect, and she will find that it is precisely that love which predisposes her for the vocation of beneficence prescribed for her by the Scriptures. There are two kinds of love: love which receives and love which gives. The former rejoices in the sentiment which it inspires and the sacrifice it obtains; the second delights in the sentiment which it experiences and the sacrifice which it makes. These two kinds of love seldom subsist apart, and woman knows them both. But is it too much to say that in her the second predominates? And that her motto, borrowed from the spontaneous love of her Savior, is "It is more blessed to give than to receive"?

To be loved! This, we well know, is the joy of a woman's heart; but alas, how often is the joy denied her! Yet let her continue to love, to consecrate herself by love; it is the exigency of her soul, the very law of her existence, a law which nothing can ever hinder her from obeying.

Man also is no stranger to this feeling. He, too, must love; but his is the love in which St. Paul sums up the obligations imposed upon the husband in conjugal life, "Husbands, love your wives," even as he sums up the duties of submission on the part of the wife: "Wives, obey your husbands." But what we are treating here is not the obligation, nor the faculty; it is the inclination to love.

Love, it must be remembered, is less spontaneous, less disinterested among men than among women. Less spontaneous in that man is often obliged to conquer himself in order to love; woman need only listen to the dictates of her innate feelings. Hence Scripture, which frequently commands the husband to love, abstains from giving this command to the wife, taking it for granted that nature herself would supply the injunction.

Moreover, the love of woman is more disinterested. Man loves woman more for his own sake than for hers; woman, on the contrary, loves man less for her own sake than for his. Man, because he is not sufficient in himself, loves that which has been given him of God; woman, because she feels that she is needed, loves him to whom God has given her. If solitude weighs heavily upon man, it is because life has no charms for him when separated from his help meet; if woman dreads living alone, it is because life has lost its aim, while she has none to whom she can be a help meet. Of her it may be said, if we may be permitted to make the comparison in the emphatic language of Scripture, "We love her because she first loved us."

If such, then, is woman's mission (and who will deny or question it?), how immensely important it is that it should be well understood, and that she should be properly trained to perform it well. But is it really understood, and is education so conducted as to qualify woman for her mission? It requires little knowledge of modern society to answer these questions in the negative.

Parents, and especially mothers, who have daughters, to you appertains the serious, deliberate, and prayerful consideration of this momentous and deeply interesting subject. Look upon those girls whom Providence has committed to your care, and say to yourselves, "I very distinctly perceive, and as impressively feel, the importance of the female character on account of its influence upon the well-being of society. And it is clear to me that woman's is a domestic mission, which is to affect society through the medium of family influence. As she fills up her place with wisdom and propriety, so will she promote the well-being of the community. Nor is it society only, but the Church of Christ, that is concerned in and promoted by the female character. Now, I have daughters who must contribute their share of influence to the public weal or woe. How shall they be educated so as best to fulfill their mission, should they be called to preside over the domestic economy? It depends much upon me whether they fail or succeed in this mission."

These are appropriate, weighty, and necessary reflections, peculiarly belonging to mothers. To them, I say, in all your conduct never let these thoughts and views be long out of your minds. Look beyond the drawing rooms of your friends, where your daughters are to be sometimes seen, perhaps shown. Look higher than to get them married, even well married. Take into account their being well-qualified to fulfill their mission. Set them before you as the future heads of a domestic establishment, and prepare them to preside over it with dignity and efficiency.

How much in modern education is calculated, if not intended, rather to prepare our females to dazzle in the circle of fashion and the lively party than to shine in the retirement of home! To polish the exterior by what are called accomplishments seems to be more the object than to give a solid substratum of piety, intelligence, good sense, and social virtue. Never was a subject less understood than education. To store the memory with facts, or to cultivate the taste for music, singing, drawing, languages, and needlework, is the ultimatum with many. The use of the intellect in the way of deep reflection, sound judgment, and accurate discrimination is not taught as it should be, while the direction of the will, the cultivation of the heart, and the formation of the character are lamentably neglected. I ask not the sacrifice of anything that can add grace, elegance, and ornament to the feminine character; but I do want incorporated with this more of what is masculine in knowledge and wisdom. I want to see woman educated not to be man's plaything, but his companion. I want to see her invested with something higher and better than fashionable littleness, elegant trifles, and fascinating airs. I want her to be fitted to hold fast her husband's heart by the esteem in which he holds her judgment; to inspire confidence and reverence in her children, and, in that home where her influence is so potent, to train up men and women who shall add to the strength and glory of the nation. In this, let mothers be assisted by those to whom they entrust the education of their daughters when they pass from their hands. It is melancholy to think of the incompetence of a large portion of those to whom the education of females is entrusted. How little has it ever occurred to many of them to inquire into woman's mission, what is necessary to qualify her for it, and how they shall aid her in obtaining this fitness! How rarely does it come within their comprehension that it is their duty, and should be their study, to impart not only knowledge, but wisdom; not only to train the performer, the artist, or the linguist, but to lay the foundation for the character of the sincere Christian, the intelligent woman, the prudent wife, the judicious mother, the sagacious mistress, and the useful member of society!

And if there is no impropriety in turning aside for a few moments to address myself as well to fathers, I would urge them to study deeply, and ponder much, the momentous importance of the domestic constitution. In the present age, how much has been said and written respecting improvements in society; but never let it be forgotten that all radical improvement must commence in the homes and hearts of our families. The inquiries how best to cure existing evils, or to supply existing defects, which do not begin here will be superficial in their nature and unsatisfactory in their results. It is in the correct understanding of the nature of parental obligations, and the right discharge of the duties of man and wife towards each other and their children, that the chief restorative remedy for the diseases of a nation must be sought, as well as the best means of preserving its health. Institutions may be set up to aid or to supplement a father's efforts, or to alter the nature or widen the sphere of woman's mission; and an artificial state of social life may be produced, varnished and glittering with the showy devices of human wisdom; but it will be found in the end that the purposes of the God of nature, the great Author of human society, cannot be frustrated, and that the parent must still be the educator of the child, and home the school for the formation of character.

And here I would remind you of your privileges as Protestants, in having no intruder thrusting himself into your families, or exerting, without coming there, through the medium of the confessional and from behind the parent's chair, an influence greater than that of the parents, whether father or mother. A French writer, Michelet, in *Priests, Women, and Families,* thus depicts the homes of his country:

> The question is about our family, that sacred asylum in which we all desire to seek the repose of the heart. We return, exhausted, to the domestic hearth; but do we find there the repose we sigh for? Let us not dissemble, but acknowledge to ourselves how things are. There is in our family a sad difference of sentiment, and the most serious of all. We may speak to our mothers, wives, and daughters on any of the subjects which form the topics of conversation with indifferent persons, such as business or the news of the day, but never on subjects that affect the heart or moral life, such as eternity, religion, the soul, and God! Choose, for instance, the moment when we naturally feel disposed to meditate with our family in common thought, some quiet evening, at the family table; venture even there, in your own house, at your own fireside, to say one word about these things. Your mother sadly shakes her head; your wife contradicts you; your daughter by her very silence shows her disapprobation. They are on one side of the table and you on the other, alone. One would think that in the midst of them, and opposite to

you, was seated an invisible personage to contradict whatever you may say.

Enter a house in the evening, and sit down at the family table; one thing will almost always strike you: the mother and daughters are together of one and the same opinion on one side, while the father is on the other side alone. What does this mean? It means that there is some one man at his table whom you do not see, to contradict and give the lie to whatever the father may utter.

Nor should young females themselves be kept in ignorance of woman's mission. Their future destiny, as stated in the last chapter, should sometimes by a wise mother or an able governess be set before them, and they themselves reminded how much is necessary on their part to prepare themselves for their future lot. They must be reminded that above and beyond accomplishments, their character is to be formed, which never can be done without their own aid. They must be early impressed—not indeed in a way to inflate their vanity, but to excite their ambition, to stimulate their energies, and to direct their aim—that they have a mission on earth, for which it becomes them most anxiously and most diligently to prepare themselves.

My young friends, let it be your constant aim, and at the same time your earnest prayer, that you may first of all thoroughly understand your mission, and then diligently prepare for it, and hereafter as successfully fulfill it. Look around and see what women commend themselves most to your judgment as worthy of imitation. You will see some, perhaps, in whom, as Monod says, reserve has degenerated into supineness, activity into restlessness, vigilance into curiosity, tact into cunning, penetration into censoriousness, promptness into levity, fluency into loquacity, grace into coquetry, taste into fastidiousness, aptitude into presumption, influence into intrigue, authority into domination, and tenderness into morbid susceptibility. In some their power of loving is converted into jealousy, and their desire for usefulness into obtrusiveness. From such turn away, as from examples in which the best qualities are metamorphosed into the worst. And equally avoid those whose whole aim seems to be to amuse and to be amused; whose vanity is predominant, even in matronly age, and who appear, in their taste for gaiety, company, and entertainments, to forget that they have any mission upon earth except to flutter in a drawing room and to dazzle its guests. On the contrary, select for your models those who seem to be aware of woman's destiny and mission, as a help meet for man.

If, in closing a chapter already too long, I may suggest a few things which, in preparing to fulfill well your future mission, it is important that you should attend to, I would mention the following:

Consider deeply that character for life is usually formed in youth. It is the golden season of life, and to none more truly and eminently so than to the young woman. Her leisure, her freedom from care, and her protected situation give her the opportunity for this, which it is her wisdom and her duty to consider, embrace, and improve.

It is of immense consequence to consider that whosoever may help you, and whatever appliances from without may be brought to bear upon your mind and heart, you must, to a considerable extent, be the constructor of your own character. Set out in life with a deep conviction of the momentous consequence of self-discipline. Let your mind, your heart, and your conscience be the chief objects of your solicitude.

Lay the basis of all your excellences in true religion, the religion of the heart, the religion of penitence, faith in Christ, love to God, a holy and heavenly mind. No character can be well-constructed, safe, complete, beautiful, or useful without this.

Cultivate those dispositions of mind which have special reference to your future mission as the help meet for man. Improve your mind, and grow in intelligence by a thirst for knowledge; for how can an ignorant woman be a companion for a sensible man? Cherish a thoughtful, reflective turn of mind. Look beneath the surface of things, beyond their present aspect to their future consequences. Be somewhat meditative, and learn to restrain your words and feelings by a rigid self-control. Pay most anxious attention to your temper, and acquire as much as possible its perfect command. More women are rendered miserable, and render others miserable, by neglect of this than perhaps from any other cause whatsoever. Let meekness of disposition and gentleness of manner be a constant study. These are woman's amiabilities, which fit her for her future situation far better than the bold, imposing, and obtrusive airs of those who mistake the secret of woman's influence.

Contentment and patience, self-denial and submission, humility and subordination, prudence and discretion are all virtues, the seeds of which you should sow in early youth so that their rich, ripe fruits might be gathered in later life. Benevolence of heart and kindness of disposition must be among your foremost studies, the most prominent objects of your pursuit and most laborious endeavors; for they are the virtues which in their maturity are to form matronly excellence, and constitute you as the fit companion for a husband.

Make accomplishments subordinate to more substantial excellences. Let the former be to the latter only as the burnish of the gold or the cutting of the diamond. And as matters of mental taste are to be less thought of than the state of the heart and the formation of moral character, so especially let bodily decorations be in low estimation compared with those of the mind.

To prepare you to carry out the duties of your future mission with ease to yourself, with satisfaction to a husband, and with comfort to a household, pay attention to the minor virtues: punctuality, love of order, and dispatch. These are all of immense importance; the want of them in the female head of a family must necessarily fill the home with confusion, and the hearts of its inmates with sadness. Set out in life with a deep conviction of the importance of habits, and a constant recollection that habits for life are formed in youth—and that these habits, if not acquired then, are likely never to be.

Aim at universal excellence. Do little things well. Avoid with extreme dread a loose, slovenly, and careless way of doing anything proper to be done.

Young woman, your whole future life will illustrate and confirm the truth and propriety of this advice, either by the comfort and usefulness which will result from your attending to it, or by the miseries which you will endure yourself and inflict on others if you allow it to sink into oblivion. It is in this way only that you can fulfill with effect that which it has been the object of this chapter to set before you: woman's mission in social life.